THE
CLINTON
SCANDALS

Political Satire in Cartoon-Illustrated Poetry

written and illustrated by

WILLIAM A. WHITAKER

Published by:

Apropos Press
PO Box 118
Smyrna, DE 19977–0118

First Edition

Printed in the United States of America by Dover Litho Printing Co., Dover, DE
Library of Congress Catalog Card Number: 98–93296

Publisher's Cataloging-in-Publication

(Prepared by Quality Books, Inc.)

Whitaker, William A.
      The Clinton scandals : political satire in
cartoon-illustrated poetry / by William A. Whitaker. —
1st ed.
      p. cm.
      Includes bibliographical references.
      Preassigned LCCN: 98–93296
      ISBN: 0–9649041–1–X

      1. Clinton, Bill, 1946– —Caricatures and cartoons.
I. Title.

E886.2.W45 1999   973.929'092
                                              QBI98–1050

For Mary

"If you look at the work that people have done in their public capacity since I have been president, you would be hard-pressed to cite examples that constitute abuse of authority."

—William Jefferson Clinton
March 1995 News Conference

CONTENTS

LIST OF ILLUSTRATIONS

All Illustrations by William A. Whitaker

THE COVER ART

The front cover of *The Clinton Scandals* is a parody of the late Grant Wood's painting "The American Gothic" from 1930. In the parody piece, the Gothic-style farmhouse is replaced by a rendition of the Classic-style White House, while the farmer-preacher and his daughter are replaced by caricatures of Bill & Hillary. This watercolor is thus, aptly entitled "The Clinton Classic."

ACKNOWLEDGEMENTS

I am grateful to my family for bearing with me through the creative times needed to write and illustrate this book. Thank you Jacki, Bill, Tim, and Brittany. A special thanks goes to my father for his proofreading assistance, and to my wife, Mary, for all her help and sacrifices.

My appreciation goes out to Joel Friedlander at Marin Bookworks and the staff at Aztec Copies for their technical contributions. For running some of the book's political cartoons on their editorial page while the issues were timely, my thanks goes out to the *Delaware State News*.

And last, but not least, I'd like to thank the Clinton Administration and the media. Their combined efforts provided a steady stream of scandals, minimizing the research necessary to write *The Clinton Scandals*.

1

BUILDING
POLITICAL
CHARACTER

THE AMERICAN
DODGER INSTITUTION

14

M y fellow Americans, I've got a song to sing
about how I became y'all's scandal king
first I shucked my morals, ethics and all
soon I was sleazin' and havin' a ball

Yeah, I dissed my scruples many year ago
learned how to sweet-talk in a day or so
and in no time I had the people of my clan
eatin' out of my hand

When it came time for chosin' my career
an' what would be perfect for someone so cavalier
I figgered this here charmer from Arkansas
would be ideally suited for practicing law

But first I'd have to get past Uncle Sam
who was recruiting young studs for Viet Nam
I cut a deal to attend an Arkansas law school
in exchange for an extended draft deferment—that was cool!

The ROTC recruiter stayed true to his pact
that he prevented my being drafted was a matter-of-fact
but I welshed on my deal, and didn't attend
I didn't break any rules; it was merely a "bend"

Then I went to Georgetown, Oxford & Yale
and tied the knot with Hillary in Fayettevaille
she was perfect for me; we's both into law
an' she gave me no grief 'bout what she never saw

I got me some weed in days gone by
my buddies & me decided to give it a try
yeah, I smoked the dope, but I later unveiled
I was within the law cuz I never inhaled

But earlier I denied to a local gazette
that I done grass in college—figgered they'd ferget
an' y'know how grass effects the memory?
they remembered real good, but what about me?

I helped a peanut farmer in his presidential bid
an' I was quite impressed with how well he did
I learned a little secret about politics:
you can get what you want if you have big bag of tricks

16

2

GENNIFER GATE

T hat very same year, I was elected AG
an' two years later the governor was me
over 'bout a dozen years, as the state's CEO
I tended to Gennifer, but who would ever know?

I never shoulda suggested to Gen that I was infertile
cuz her protection got spotty—then she was with chil'
I gave her the money to make the problem go away
an' as soon as she recovered we continued to play

Gen's apartment was close to the mansion of the guv
and when she spotted me joggin' from a balcony up above
she propped open a side door so I could slip on in
and rendezvous together in our secret worlds of sin

I employed a State Trooper to make my joggin' look legit
after I finished at Genny's pad, I engaged in a little skit
I'd give L.D. a phone call, asking him to pick me up
at another location I jogged to, feigning I was a tired pup

3

BUILDING POLITICAL CLOUT

L.D. had drug enforcement background on his resumé
so I encouraged him to apply for work with the C.I.A.
then I slipped him into a remote contraband arena
of money, guns and drugs thru an airport known as Mena

I teamed him up with Barry, a controversial pilot for the D.E.A.
who parachuted into Central America an arms caché
they returned home with 2 duffel bags full of money & cocaine
instead of becoming a narc, L.D. had become a conspirator to the game

When L.D. protested to me about the exchanging of contraband
I explained to him that the deal belonged to my buddy Dan
Dan is a felon, but since he gives me financial campaign support
I look the other way while he gets rich in his illegal sport

Dan received cocaine jail time, but after 6 months got probation
I gave him my personal pardon, compliments of my administration
Barry got sentenced for drug dealing in both '85 & '86
with no mention of the Mena activities—I've got a bottomless bag of tricks

Barry had smuggled drugs into the U.S. to 'bout the $5 billion range
and L.D. became concerned that this would never change
but a new C.I.A. employee, Felix, insisted there was nothing to fear
then Barry was silenced permanently as he entered a halfway house that year

I promised L.D. an appointment to a position at the State Crime Lab
felt if I made him Assistant Director, I could trust him not to blab
I changed my mind, welshed on the deal, and lost him as a friend
but he still held dirt on me, from which I preferred not to defend

I asked for L.D.'s help again when he was Prez of the Police Association
I needed the cops' support for a tax increase legislation
in return I pledged legislation for a State Police pay raise
the cops came through, but I welshed again—contributing to more malaise

L.D. told the press I reneged on the pay raise pledge
I figured I'd be much better off without this dividing wedge
so I worked out a few differences with this hard-to-please son-of-a-gun
and the cops got their pay raise bill in 1991

Then Arkansas employee, Larry, was charging personal toll calls to the state
because he abused his privileges, I decided termination was his fate
Larry retaliated—he filed a defamation suit against me
in which he charged that I was using state funds to finance my adultery

The state funded my affairs, according to Larry's suit,
with multiple unnamed women (and believe me they were cute)
for five other state-funded lovers, he provided each and every name
one of which was Gennifer, the suit happened to proclaim

All those state scandals Larry exposed turned out to be my OJT
and this political on-the-job training would ultimately benefit me
it gave me plenty of practice—*denying allegation after allegation*
which proved to be critical preparation for my running the nation

4

TROOPER GATE

26

While I was campaigning for guv in '78
Hillary dabbled in cattle futures, and she done just great!
she started with a thousand dollars in her hand
after nine months of "abracadabras" she held 100 grand

As guv in the 80s, I made only 35 thou per year
so to secure 400K in unsecured loans, I needed a special financier
the local bankers took care of me; and they couldn't be ignored
so I appointed one *the banking commissioner,* sort of a little reward

We been a one-party state since the Civil War days
and while the Repubs are away, Arkansas plays
in commerce, justice and politics we scratch each others backs
all funded by the poor when they pay their tax

I bragged that I was the lowest paid guv in the nation
but auditor Julia made the revelation
that the state's been footin' the annual bill
for my perks, benefits & abuse for 3/4 mill

OK, in our oligarchal state we play by different rules
me & my buddies had the power, funded by our fools
our symbiotic relationships rendered us innocent of any crime
it seems like mostly da po fokes be da ones dat's doin' time

When I pulled strings, 'bout anything could get done
and among other things, I's havin' lots of fun
I was a modern day Willie from *All the King's Men*
'cept I planned to survive the state for the Washington den

An '88 presidential bid didn't sound bad
but I's a little concerned about all the liaisons I'd had
so I hired Betsey as a guardian against bimbo eruption
then axed my plan to run cuz I's buried in corruption

I was tryin' to suppress stories on Troopergate
where I had cops guardin' my door when ladies were in real late
don't get me wrong now; they were strictly business dealin's
'twas merely emotional chats that caused the moans, groans an' squealin's

I kinda felt bad 'bout the troopers at the door
'cuz playin' like wooden soldiers had to be a bore
I decided to reward them for securin' my rendezvous
by inviting extra women so the guards could partake too

Gen & I were on a videotape made by her next door neighbor, Gary
so to eliminate the evidence, there arose a mercenary
who beat Gary senseless and left him for dead
the video tape disappeared while Gary bled

5

PAULA GATE

I said goodbye to Genny in '89
for a dozen-year lover, she done jes' fine
but cuz I'm so handsome & the guv
I can get 'em much younger; and that's what I luv

Hey, hey Paula, wanna meet me in the hotel?
hey Paula, you have to promise not to tell
the fire I had for her she quickly extinguished
but not before she saw how I was very distinguished

Through selective amnesia I lost all my memory
of this aborted sexual encounter between Paula & me
but she remembered real good, and chose to file a suit
when the high court acquiesced, she no longer looked so cute

She thought that 'cuz I dropped my trousers I was overly crude
but you don't meet me in my private room and suddenly turn prude
Paula wanted me to admit what I did, and she even made it easy
she asked for a real apology, but I didn't want to come off sleazy

Armed with creative writing skills, I decided to have some fun
I claimed to have no recollection of meeting her in my room in 1991
I didn't challenge having met her there or meeting her in the past
but when I cleared her of any sexual misconduct, she said *not so fast*

Paula said she was grateful I acknowledged that we may have met
on May 8th in the Excelsior Hotel (how could I forget?)
but on showing her my privates, she stood behind her claim
so we had reached an impasse; it really was a shame

I've never been one to apologize; I guess it's 'cuz I'm vain
plus in acquiescing her request, I'd have nothing to gain
it would be David against Goliath if her case was tried
but how was I to know it would be my political suicide

6

THE BOOMER PRESIDENT

I 'd become the Teflon no-stick Houdini of scandal
'cuz there appeared to be no corruption I couldn't handle
I's wastin' my talent down in Arkansas
figgered now I'd run for prez . . . & shoot for it all

They said I let a chicken giant pollute Arkansas streams
but Don was a staunch supporter of all my political dreams
I wouldn't prosecute someone who helped bankroll me
so let the coliform grow; I plan to be in DC

I got the '92 Democratic nomination
they figgered I's the guy to lead the nation
but when I got campaignin', things started lookin' bleak
I got haunted by my past—I had a scandal every week

The scandals gave me plenty of reason to fear
that perhaps my run for prez wouldn't work that year
but golly! I was blessed by a wild card candidate
he took votes from the Repubs, & I was in for eight

I truly had a pop culture inauguration
befitting for the first boomer to head the nation
my glorification bashes were Hollywoodian strong
but the *thousand dollar seats* from a liberal I guess was wrong

I raised my hand; they swore me in
my new reign of corruption was about to begin:
I started downsizin' the Travel Office; ended up cleanin' house
then backfilled with my cronies . . . an' they called me a louse?

The people loved me anyway, as they done since I's a scholar
I made 'em think I saw it their way; then I make 'em holler
I told the little folks I'd raise taxes only on the rich
but once I's voted into office I did a little switch

As a candidate I described the rich as those makin' 200K per year
when I became the President I switched it to the 100 thousand tier
then my White House aid said we'd draw the line at thirty
so alas! We made the middle class rich, and you thought that I played dirty?

7

THE HEALTH CARE SCANDAL

I llegals were gettin' free health care, while many citizens had to pay
so I decided to take advantage of the resulting affray
to consider a plan to cover legal citizens as well
I created a health reform task force; Hillary was head mademoiselle

She had no medical background, but she was my #1 crony
I figgered y'all'd go for her plan, even if it was phony
but Congress wasn't blind, and gave the plan the axe
'bout her $13.8 million budget overrun—you weren't supposed know those facts

Bill HR 3600 was to make our medicine socialized
it would have taken away discretionary doctor visits—they'd have to be
        authorized
through one of 60 new bureaucracies that the health plan would create
employing 50,000 more government workers—it would've been just great

And participation was to be compulsary for citizens like you and you
but we'd have exempted the president, congressman, and their families, just
        to name a few
before we included ourselves, we wanted to ensure it proved a success
why include high ranking government officials if it turns out a mess?

I would have been involved in the administration of the plan
through a seven member review board, appointed by the man
the man of course is me, and you know what that would have meant?
more opportunity for abuse of power from your President

It would've been against the law to get insurance outside our plan
you & your doctor couldn't choose your services; only the government can
the Feds would've rationed health care according to "global budget constraints"
I can't imagine a system like this ever getting any complaints

You'd have had to wait your turn for services, even if the wait might cause
        you to die
and the Feds would've controlled medical education—to prevent it from going
        awry
they'd have limited young doctors seeking specialty training to 45%
and race & ethnicity would've been factored into who was actually sent

Abortion on demand for a $10 copayment, and condoms given out in schools
this would have been a beautiful plan after we'd rewritten the medical rules
your government issued ID cards would open your files for anyone to see
since you shouldn't have nothin' to hide, you'd have gotten no privacy

8

MENDING (NOT ENDING) AFFIRMATIVE ACTION

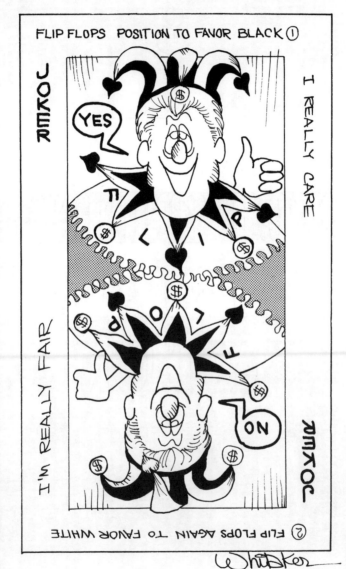

When it came to supportive constituents, I knew the closets were full
of gay & lesbian Americans, and I figgered I could use their pull
when AIDS blew the closet doors open, I quelled a gay pell-mell
by creatin' a military policy that I coined "don't ask, don't tell"

Affirmative action created a syndrome—*the angry white males*
but I needed diversity votes lest my reelect bid fails
to appease the angry white guys, I pledged a fix after a review
but my "mend don't end" fixed nothing—another promise gone askew

A white teacher got laid off, while a black woman got to stay
George's administration had backed the white woman from Piscataway
but I flip-flopped his position, to show the blacks I really care
then I flip-flopped once again to show the whites I'm really fair

The office of Air Force Secretary had never been held by a black
so I nominated a senator named Daryl to put us on the diversity track
they blasted my fellow Democrat for exaggerating the truth
but deception is a good quality—and I'm the living proof

He embellished the number of flying hours he'd actually had
and claimed his grounding was voluntary, not 'cuz his flying was bad
but a superior explained that he was grounded for poor performance in the air
the scrapes he left on his aircraft had given Colonel Tom a scare

Daryl accepted extra flight pay while he was working on the ground
but are all these factors relevant if you're Air Force Secretary bound?
I was disappointed he got rejected, in part, for his propensity to lie
but as long as he's serving as Secretary, he wouldn't be a threat to our sky

9

THE
POLITICAL
STRATEGIST

W hen Dick & I met we was both in our twunnies
he shared my passion for glitz, gals & moneys
he told me I could reach the top under his advisory
and his strategies were quite palatable—he was principle-free

With him in my corner, I always seemed to win
so I funded his life of luxury—it really was a sin
until he crossed me up one day, and it was brought to light
that he was sharing Presidential strategies with a lady-of-the-night

While Dick was my consultant we had a little clash
he insisted that for me to be reelected required a little cash
"little" sounded OK, but I had to swallow the bitter pill
what he wanted me to spend on advertising was about 85 mill

To obtain federal matching funds, I agreed to spend only 37 mill
but my reelection required much, much more, so I used DNC's till
sure the practice is illegal; soft money is for party use
but when my authorized funds proved not ample, the party turned their
    money loose

The Repubs regained the Senate & House, then the media blitz began
although integrity can't get me reelected, lotsa money can
I was quite thankful to Dick about how the election went
but how could I ever repay all the money we spent?

Janet opened a 1998 inquiry into my ad campaign
I'd funneled 42 mill in party funds and she wanted me to explain
why I'd accepted millions in matching funds to the tune of 13.4
after pledging to spend what was authorized, and not one cent more

10

LIQUIDATING CAMPAIGN DEBTS

I needed a viable plan for campaign debt liquidation
but to avoid another scandal, it needed obfuscation
I assigned the task to Ron, an exfundraiser for the DNC
who secretly ran an outpost from the office of Commerce Secretary

The press said I overran the Commerce Department with political appointees
and campaign donors were rewarded by my first two Commerce Secretaries
with seats on trade missions and other generous perks
I's only playin' politics, and that's basically how it works

Ron died a traumatic death when he went down in a plane
sparing him the testimony in which he was to explain
to an Independent Counsel all his financial dealings
but for an admissible seance, there'd be no posthumous squealings

A Military Medical Examiner later made the claim
that though dead at the crash site, a bullet could be to blame
a suspicious round hole located at the top of Ron's head
aroused theories that a 45 caliber slug was the reason he was dead

Conspiracy theorists suggested the Democrats silenced Ron
'cuz he wouldn't be able to talk after he was gone
about the White House officials who'd given him instructions
to withhold incriminating documents—your basic justice obstruction

The documents were evidence that I was exchanging trade mission seats
for Democratic contributions—who, ME involved in deceit?
I figured I was in the clear once Ron was in his grave
but Nolanda exposed the scheme; can't anybody behave?

Ron was under White House pressure, she testified to the court
to cover up this scandal by withholding any incriminating document or report
Leon & John instructed Ron, she went on to testify
to withhold the evidence till after the election, which the White House did deny

When it came to raising money I really had no match
I could make small fortune at a White House coffee klatsch
or I could do some *dialing for dollars* from my White House home
I figgered the donors were legal from the other end of the phone

The klatsches were no big deal—103 java sessions in all
besides, the $27 million we raised was relatively small
and we didn't call 'em fund raisers—but merely "fund raising dates"
if you flashed an open checkbook we'd let you through our gates

Although it's prohibited on federal property
Al did a few fundraising solicitations for me
from the White House phone, he solicited across the land
and in some 56 calls, he yielded nearly 700 grand

Al's a skilled magician; he performed magic for me
got $5000 donations from Buddhists who'd vowed their poverty
he's also a talented cleaner; he laundered that money
and gave the laundered $140,000 to the DNC

The temple reimbursed the monks for the money they'd donated
in an illegal fund-rasing scheme the Democrats had orchestrated
Maria got indicted for hiding illegal campaign contributions
taking the hit for Al; saving him from prosecution

While Maria took the heat, Al stayed on the loose
if you're the nation's #2 man, ignorance is a good excuse
he didn't know it was a fundraiser; he called it a "donor-maintenance event"
and raising Democratic funds was its primary intent

Al doesn't have my teflon coating, but still he's slicker than most
he's got a few scandals of his own about which he can boast
he's gotta stay in practice of sleazing with a straight face
so when I leave the oval office, he can take my place

A memorial fund in Al's sister's name received two $50 grand donations
donor, *Molten Metal, was rewarded 2 days later* became an accusation
their government-funded research was increased from one million bucks to ten
Molten donated to the DNC the day the government expanded their yen

The press was really scruitinizin' our fund raisin' strategy
then George, one of my ex-cronies started workin' part time for ABC
he arranged a mayoral fundraiser at 25 hundred bucks a head
it was OK by my standards, but the network put it to bed

11

WHITE HOUSE PAY-PER STAYS

After I created a White House policy called "pay per stay"
I couldn't keep the wealthy entrepreneurs away
but in assigning the rented rooms I had to be discreet
so da mo' money day paid, da better da suite

The lure of stayin' in Abe's bedroom made my pay-per-stay a hit
but not all my clientele wanted an overnight visit
I didn't want to lose a donation from any wealthy White House patron
so I added an adventurous contingency: a ride on Air Force One

Yup, the prez is for sale today
rooms for rent—about 50K
most Americans can't afford that kinda dough
but the Asians seized the opportunity and the money began to flow

An Asian-American businessman gave us Dems 360K in money
after we scrutinized the dough, we figgered it was a little funny
under media fire, we turned it back, sayin' we didn't know its source
but we'd cleared Johnny's 50 White House visits cuz money talks of course

Johnny also disguised a bribe with my Energy Secretary
he donated $25,000 to her favorite charity
Hazel was then very quick to arrange
a meeting with a Chinese petrochemical rep in exchange

On exchanging access for the donation, Hazel claimed *no way!*
despite the fact that they both took place on the very same day
and since she's on the board of directors of the that charitable organization
she fit quite well in the scheme of things with my administration

It was a good thing that Janet was there to let her off the hook
Hazel was unaware her group got the money—she ain't no crook
when I appointed Janet AG, I knew what I's doin'
We can break all the rules we want, cuz we're prosecution immune

Hillary likes to throw an extravagant Christmas bash
but extravagance can exceed the budgeted cash
so rather than compromise the lavishness & glitz
Maggie took Johnnie's check for 50K to offset the debits

I gave another Asian John a political appointment because
when I was runnin' for prez he donated to my cause
we allowed him 94 white house visits; but visits ain't no crimes
besides he only saw me 'bout 15 times

Then there was an Indonesian banker, an' boy he gave us plenty
I acknowledged a few of his White House visits, but my aids said
    "more like twenty"
but James' visits were purely social; so what if he paid?
and so what if, while he was here, we discussed some Asian trade?

12

SHOW ME THE MONEY

E nter generous Charlie, a restauranteur from Little Rock
we returned $645K to him he'd raised from the Asian block
under allegations of working for the Chinese and also having spied
he disappeared to Beijing, insisting he had "nothing to hide"

I granted Roger a meeting following his $300 K donation
I gladly accepted the cash-for-access despite the violation
after I ignored his Caspian oil pipeline pitch, he said he should have given six
if he'd have given it in the first place, he might not have been in this fix

Warren made a $5 million campaign offer with potential of another fifty
funneled through several tax-exempt groups—what the hell? We're already shifty!
to enable his donations to be deductible, the White House sent him a fax
listing organizations supporting me, that would exempt his contributions from tax

Harry called Warren from Air Force One and asked for one & a half mill
wanting the dough in 24 hours—a kind of tough order to fill
he then asked Warren to shred the fax—it was erroneously sent
but I still would like money he pledged; every dollar and cent

Many of the funds we raised were boomerang donations
2 million of this funny money was returned by my administration
The Senate questioned donors about being reimbursed for what they'd given
a practice that has worked for us since we became money driven

A trade problem was costing FedEx $100 million per year
so I met, one-on-one with the CEO, and lent him my ear
but Freddie knows the rules: nobody sees me for free
then he & his delivery company donated $275 K to the DNC

Unsuccessful union challenger James made some allegations
that the Teamsters and the Democrats were illegally trading donations
Rich's memo asking them *to steer a million bucks to us* was brought to light
'twas a brilliant scheme to fetch big money without a White House invite

I gave Rich, a retired banker, a dialing-for-dollars call
he claims it came from the White House, but of course I can't recall
everybody remembers things I don't, but it doesn't make me sweat
when questioned about the things I've done, it's convenient to forget

I figgered I'd be a hero, and support a change in the FEC
that would ban these big dollar contributions coined *soft money*
this way no future candidate for a political office run
will be able to rake in funny money the way that I have done

I later changed my mind on banning soft money donations
'cuz I still had a couple more years to head the nation
why should I eliminate a funding source that's totally unregulated
at a time when the incoming funds keeps me inundated

So I came up with a brand new brainstorm
I suggested we have campaign finance reform
I know that ignorance of the law is never an excuse
but me & my cronies are quite obtuse

13

FUND RAISING INVESTIGATIONS

THE PREZ HUGGING ILLEGAL CONTRIBUTORS: THE STORY BEHIND THE STORY

As a result of all the fund raising allegations
the RNC wanted a special prosecutor's investigation
but Janet refused to appoint counsel—my Democratic protective shroud
a cozy conflict of interest of which I'm quite proud

After many gave testimony indicating fund raising violations
Janet opened a 30-day review in response to the allegations
Hell, it's my White House SOP; why are we under attack?
it cost me a fortune to get elected; I only want to get it back

The White House got subpoenaed in February
for any & all coffee and fund raising material—kinda scary!
we had some video tapes that we didn't want y'all to see
so Lanny said they did not exist—straight-faced, just like me

Janet said, regarding the White House coffees, she saw no illegality
then the very next day we announced our startling discovery
we "found" 44 video tapes of these klasches hosted by me
we'd have produced them much sooner but they were being edited, you see?

It was really an accident that they took 8 months to find
I was hopin' ya'll would say "oh never mind"
but instead, we hear this "obstruction of justice" whining
suggesting we intentionally withheld evidence of our donation-dining

One tape showed five checks bein' offered to Dan
after which he said "as soon as this thing is over . . ." Oh what a man!
another showed me meeting with John, a fundraiser renowned
good thing that on that tape our editor deleted the sound

Surprise! We had another hundred-hours on tape—the evidence was growing
we'd have turned 'em over sooner, but for our private White House showing
after which Lanny assured the public that all the events were squeaky clean
but I shouldn't have hugged & praised illegal contributors on the video screen

After the Republicans put our fund raising under close scrutiny
We were unable to reduce the $15 million debt of the DNC
so we invited generous Democrats who had 50 grand to spare
to a Florida weekend with Al & me—at a price we thought was fair

As we kicked off the weekend of gluttony, among other sins
I said the party with the most money is the one that wins
for their generosity, the schmoozers got a bargain of sorts
I couldn't do any talking, cuz I was a little hoarse

After hearing testimony of all the shady stuff we did
and viewing all the cash-for-klatsch tapes, however lurid
Fred ended the finance-abuse probe after 32 days
proving that I can get away with anything; so why change my ways?

The Justice Department's Task Force's recommendation to Janet
for the *Fundraising Independent Counsel decision* was for her to can it
Al & I were pleased we survived our indiscretionary scrapes
I wonder if they still wanna see these extra 26 tapes

She rationalized the calls I made were from the residential wing
which is anywhere I want it to be—it didn't mean a thing
she concluded that the DNC improperly got the dough
from Al's White House solicitations, but Al's OK cuz he didn't know

A subpoena for Louis' & Charles' memos eventually gave the table a turn
but Janet refused to comply—she didn't want Al to burn
The Government Reform & Oversight Committee then voted to
hold her in contempt of Congress—so what's she gonna do?

The memos contained recommendations for Janet to name
an outside counsel instead of hiding the blame
she claimed releasing the memos could bring the probe some devastation
that's a pretty good line, and I must admit I was impressed by her evasion

Janet will always take care of me, you have to understand
after I read her FBI files, my wish became her command
Jack, a high profile Florida attorney brought this stuff to light
that the goods I had on her included her using ladies-of-the-night

Jack claims that Janet fears something more than my wrath
who, me allow closet skeletons to destroy her AG aftermath?
I'll keep the closet door closed as long as she takes care of me
but if Jack turns loose his evidence, it'll still taint her legacy

Although Janet didn't like the contempt cloud hanging over her head
she still didn't appoint counsel; she opened a 90-day exam instead
for Al, this was 90-day examination by the Justice Department #2
when you're part of my administration, you have to expect a few

Janet then focused on Harold, whose earlier testimony
might not have been the whole truth; possibly bologna
since this former White House aid had been groomed by me
he knew that the best defense for dishonor was a good dose of perjury

14

RANKING PROFIT OVER NATIONAL SECURITY

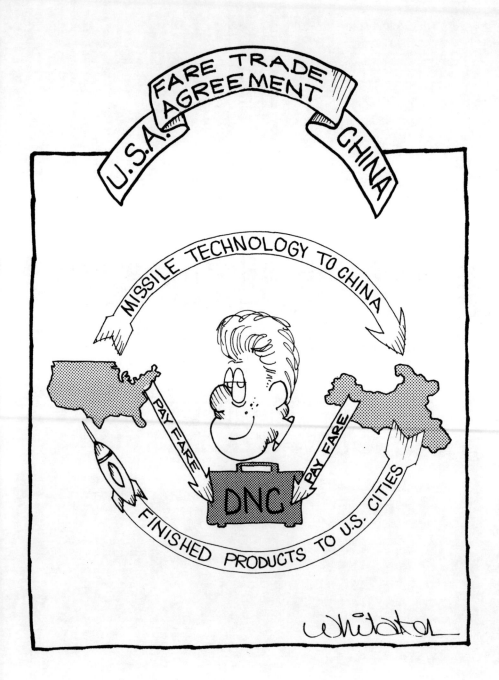

Then Johnny broke the story about his donation of $100 grand
it originated from a Chinese military officer who had put it in his hand
the instructions were to allocate it to the various Democratic campaigns
but rumor had it we gave the Chinese missile technology in exchange

After Bernard wrote a hundred grand check to the DNC
he was included on a trade mission organized by the Commerce Secretary
Ron whisked him off to China to meet the Communications Minister
the dealings for Loral were very good; but for the US—sinister

The Justice Department initiated a probe of my administration
after we allowed 2 US firms to export satellites to the Chinese nation
the Repubs think these waivers allowed the Chinese to gain nuclear technology
that they later sent to Pakistan, testing Indian psychology

This could have pushed India forward, leading to its own nuclear tests
we shouldn't have exported the technology, culminating in this mess
but since Bernard, chairman of one of the firms we'd given the waiver to,
donated $632 grand to the Democratic Party, we had to push it through

After getting them the Asian money, the Democrats abandoned me:
The House & Senate voted to block future satellite exports, overwhelmingly
they wanted to bar any future agreements I have with the Chinese
involving space or missile-related technology cuz my past deals reeked of sleaze

The GOP called for cancellation of my scheduled China trip
but I wouldn't bow to political pressure—come on, get a grip!
I wanted to thank the Chinese on their home turf for their loyalty
for being so generous when buying influence—they knew it wasn't free

Bernard insisted that Loral's China deal was clean as a whistle
the deal that resulted in "made in America" printed on each Chinese missile
and the missiles could very well be aimed at major cities in the USA
shucks, ranking profit over national security is becoming the American way

Since I've been in office, Bernard's given the Democrats over a million dollars
so, in determining who gets favorable treatment, it doesn't take Rhodes scholars
and when the Chinese decide to nuke our cities with US acquired technology
I'll let y'all know the targets in advance for a generous donation to the DNC

But national security is something I've always tended to compromise
when there's potentional for corporate advances, I favor the enterprise
national security doesn't donate money the way large corporations do
I'm willing to do the same for others as I did for Loral and Hughes

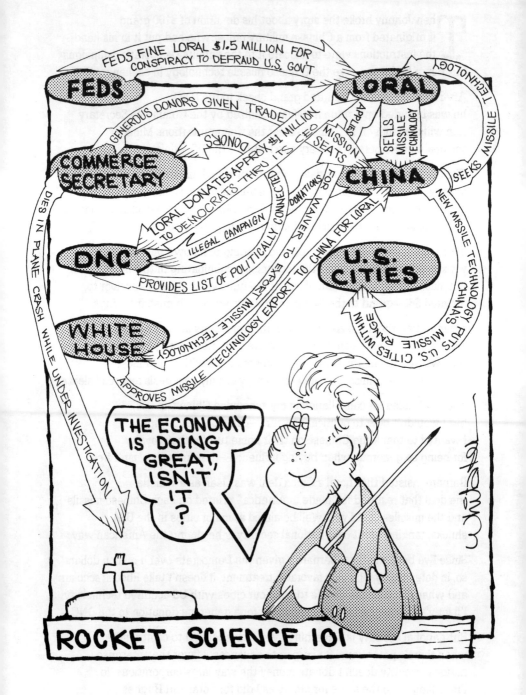

THE TIANANMEN
SQUARE-DANCE

69

After easing the controls on supercomputer sales in 1995
I might have put our national security into a nose dive
Russia purchased 17 computers for a nuke lab
but IBM flourished from the 2 million dollar tab

15

CASINO GATE

A casino was proposed by 3 Chippewa tribes
so they could make money off anyone who imbibes
after an opposing tribe hired a Democratic lobbyist, we gave the
Chippewa plan the axe
their opponents' $270 grand DNC donation influenced the casino rejection
climax

The victimized tribes claimed *only Democratic donors get government aid*
cuz the ones gettin' federal help are the ones that have paid
and the unfortunate ones cry foul, like the one from Washington state
makin' a big fuss about my vacationing on my friend's Richard's estate

They concluded my staying on his Martha's Vineyard spread
convinced me to favor a tribe with whom Richard was connected
so when Bruce acquiesced the wishes of the well-connected tribe
the $2 million in Indian donations we received started lookin more like bribes

The Republicans requested Independent Counsel for this major act of sleaze
which allowed the Injuns with the most money to 'bout get anything they please
but Janet could reject the request for counsel with her standard rubber stamp
it's so nice to have an Attorney General from the Democratic camp

A cronie was at stake in this appointment-of-Independent-Counsel push
and only I was capable of saving Brucie's little tush
by merely asking special consideration from my conflict-of-interest A.G.
she could refuse to appoint the counsel, and Bruce would be home free

But Janet was gettin' tired of taking flack for my acts of sleaze
like withholding fund-raising tapes from her, and my other dishonesties
and I was so busy covering up for my sexual indescretions
that I never asked her to protect Bruce from the unfortunate processions

After Janet requested Independent Counsel, Brucie vowed to fight
no counsel had been appointed for my fundraisers—this certainly wasn't right
he predicted he would win, but it didn't really matter to me
heck, they can send all my cronies to jail, as long as I'm home free

16

USER-FRIENDLY IRS

After much testimony exposed abuses from the IRS
a citizen's oversight board was proposed by Congress
Gene vowed to oppose such a group's creation
why should we protect the taxpayers of our nation?

I agreed with my adviser: the IRS need not change
cuz I get treated quite well in my income range
plus they add a perk to the Feds, although it's quite sad:
we can sic 'em on you any time we want, if you make us mad

But the public's trust in IRS continued to slide
and soon it was obvious that I was on the wrong side
so from my creative juices came a brainstorm
to flip flop my position and support the reform

The Senate approved the overhaul bill overwhelmingly
to remove the terror from our tax collection agency
after arguing on the other side, it made me feel a little ill
that I had to vacillate my position before signing the reform bill

17

MY NOT-SO-PRIVATE EXTRAMARITAL AFFAIRS & UNDERWEAR

80

I wanted the young Americans to relate better to me
so I made a national appearance on MTV
I had a hard time maintaining my cool and debonair
as a young girl asked me about my underwear

The military started cleanin' house of promiscuity
funny how ever'one then started lookin' over ta me
Hell, I'll admit I'm a ladies' man; and sometimes even a toad
but I play by my own standards, not by military code

Along came a prosecutin' specialist who went by the name of Kenny
askin' bodyguards about my affairs; it's no secret there were plenty
Kenny's staff insisted he was building a proper case
But I think he's hittin' below the belt investigatin' leather & lace

So in order to shirk Kenny on these promiscuity things
I had to silence the ladies claiming we had intimate flings
like high school sweetheart, Dolly—we were an item for years
at least that's what she would claim if you lent her your ears

She wrote an account about our trist, in a fictionalized book
but since she was basing it on fact, my camp got a little shook
Purposes of the Heart, because of threats and intimidation
was blocked from being published—and she blamed my administration

She gave me an ultimatum: settle up or face a suit
she might as well just sue me 'cuz I ain't givin' her my loot
I'll make sure the case is heard by a judge appointed by me
so we can have it thrown out—reciprocation from a crony

18

BUILDING A DIVERSE CABINET

I pledged to make my cabinet look like the country in which we live
but I started losing my early picks like water through a sieve
just as well, I'd make more picks; figgered society might not enjoy
havin' a cabinet made up of people with illegal aliens in their employ

I painted my cabinet colorfully; Van Gogh would have been proud
but by trading competence for diversity, I created a thunder cloud
many ended up under fire, but what do you expect?
the cabinet looks like America, and America ain't perfect

My Agriculture Secretary, Mike, was an Arkansas good ol' boy
who received from chicken king Don, nice gifts to enjoy
he got a 39 count indictment for benefiting from companies under his regulation
I was surprised he had resigned; it's my style of compensation

Senior Sun Diamond VP Richard pleaded guilty to bribing Mike
with goods & perks worth $7500; stuff he knew Mike would like
he wanted his firm to win favor with me and my administration
he should have given it directly to me to save the aggravation

Independent Counsel, Donald, convicted Mike's boss, Ron
the Justice Department had objected; didn't want their man a con
and Ron was only guilty of lying to hide $22 grand he'd gotten
from agri businesses while he's the chief of staff—how rotten

Alexis gave me diversity points when I appointed her Secretary of Labor
she'd recently sold her consulting firm to a close friend & neighbor
Vanessa's consulting firm soon flourished with success
due to connections at the White House thanks to Alexis

Allegations surfaced indicating that Alexis was on the take
for 10% of any consulting fees that Vanessa should happen to make
I don't believe these allegations—not even for a minute
she'd never be in a kickback scheme without including me in it

In the Democratic scheme of things, for success one must pay
so Vanessa & her sister engaged in a $250,000 give-away
the Democratic Party gladly accepted their donations
which made them all fat & happy through financial-symbiotic-relations

After her accuser, Laurent, blew the whistle on the Labor Chief
a preliminary inquiry commenced to see if she was an influence peddling thief
Janet determined that Laurent's story had enough corroboration
to seek independent counsel—chalk up another for the administration

For my Secretary of State, I wanted someone born abroad
I wanted that someone to be a woman, so the feminists would applaud
and for more diversity points, I wanted this person to be a Jew
We hadn't had one since Henry, and this pick would make just two

My new Secretary of State was Madeleine—Prague was her birth place
she came with a strong resumé—no chance for my disgrace
in a previous post at the United Nations, she'd really done quite well
but her oblivion to her own Jewish heritage was a little hard to sell

The office of Surgeon General became my hornets' nest
cuz I stuck with a criteria of *diversity* instead of with the *best*
enter Jocelyn, bless her soul, who got the confirmation
but I had to send her sailin' when she started talkin' *masturbation*

Then there was the abortion problem with my nominee named Henry
couldn't remember the number he'd performed—he's challenged by his memry
so it took me 'bout three years to find a doctor to head our nation
hard to find anybody qualified who fits my discrimination

Another Arkansas good ol' boy became my nominee
for the Secretary of Veterans Affairs, his name was Hershey
but with sexual misconduct charges standing in his way
Hersh withdrew from consideration—another spoils candidate slipped away

It's embarrassing when my nominees fall through the cracks
I'll admit Hersh didn't look so good considering his background facts
but I can't nominate the best with a criterion of a *crony* or *diversity*
figgered I stand a better chance with the incumbent Army Secretary

19

THE ARLINGTON FLAP

S o I nominated Togo, a much stronger candidate
I actually wanted y'all to approve him before I nominate
I know it's a tad irregular, but I didn't want a media blast
for losing another nominee cuz of skeletons in his past

The GOP charged he approved burial plots for Democratic donors,
the Arlington flap made out to be one of our political boners
so what if a contributor got a veteran's plot as a donation fringe?
the draft-dodging exception-granting prez is what really makes vets cringe!

But Larry raised over $10 million for the Democrats over the years
he gave $200 grand to our campaign, fortifying Al's & my careers
so he fabricated a little story about being torpedoed while at sea
the tale was good enough for Togo, and it was good enough for me

OK, he wasn't in the armed forces, but he claimed a Merchant Marine
and he wasn't on the manifest of the ship hit by the submarine
we don't look gift horses in the mouth, so we didn't investigate his claim
which was exposed as fabricated honors; it really was a shame

His widow, Shiela, was surprised with the revelation
which was initially trashed as *Insight's* unsubstantiated allegation
so when the truth was unearthed about the scam for his Arlington plot
she had him moved to a different cemetery—he was taking a veterans spot

His headstone read "S1C Merchant Marine"; can you believe he had the nerve
to claim he was a seriously wounded veteran when he didn't even serve?
he was buried in one of the last 50 plots in coveted section 7A
in the company of Medal of Honor earning heros who didn't have to pay

I admit I appointed Larry our Ambassador to Switzerland
but let me dispel the rumors: I was never Shiela's man
It was written that considering his appointment, Larry would look the other way
whenever Sheila and I decided to go astray

I denied the sexual charges, and Shiela did too
she filed three $25 million lawsuits, and eventually dropped two
she wanted to hold a columnist accountable for her claim
that in exchange for Larry's ambassadorship she became my flame

I appointed him ambassador because of his generosity
the funding was that important to Al & me
but he didn't know Switzerland was neutral—thought it was a U.S. ally
I figgered *what the hell, with a little on-the-job training he'd eventually qualify*

And Larry wasn't special; other burial waivers were given by me
I gave one to a former Surgeon General who hadn't even donated heavily to
     the DNC
I merely wanted to repay C. Everett for supporting Hillary's failing Health Care
     Plan
although her health bill went belly-up, I still wanted to compensate this man

We rushed to get the waiver through in 1994
for his 8/17 White House arrival—we got it the day before
but by 1998, the bearded-one surrendered his Arlington burial rights
after news of my slick arrangements had come to the public light

I was trying to set a precedent for non-vets who practiced stroking me
to show them that military service is optional at Arlington Cemetery
you see, never before had a living non-vet been awarded burial rights
at the Arlington Cemetery, but of course I thought those rules were trite

20

EXTREMIST MARINES & OTHER SCANDALS

T ogo worked closely with Sara, the Assistant Army Secretary
I appointed her to that position to enhance the diversity
she was the top Personnel Officer for Manpower and Reserve Affairs
but when she called the Marines "extremists", she ruffled many hairs

While pumping up the Army, she established her notoriety
by indicating the Marines were less connected to society
she also mocked the Marine uniforms, calling them *checkerboard, fancy & stuff*
then resigned in the wake of the furor she caused; the Marines had heard enough

Y'all think I dishonored my country when I dodged the military draft
and when I stuffed Democratic coffers with illegal foreign cash
and when I exported missile technology, jeapordizing national security
so does it surprise you when I court-martial citizens for honoring their country?

Army Specialist Michael was court-martialed by my administration
for refusing to be an involuntary mercenary for the United Nations
he was ordered to wear the U.N.'s patch and its headgear colored blue
but he chose to maintain a singular U.S. loyalty, protecting citizens like you

When Michael refused to obey the orders, we screwed him really good
for his failure to serve under foreign flags, like a scumbag traitor would
and, yes, we're in default on our U.N. dues—the U.S. ain't paid 'em in years
but, no, they'll never court-martial me for being in arrears

A Texan named David headed a cultist community
the group seemed to be living in an eccentric harmony
but the Feds disliked their weapons and their fortified compound
so Janet ordered a raid, and it burnt to the ground

Ever' time I had a scandal fix all but figgered out
another skeleton from my closet came a jumpin' out
I decided I'd take all these hits without payin' an attorney fee
by creatin' a defense fund in '94, 'specially for me

21

THE HUSH MONEY HUD SECRETARY

96

Housing & Urban Development needed diversity
so I appointed to Secretary, a Hispanic named Henry
but during his background check, word was that he lied
what could the ex-mayor of San Antonio possibly have to hide?

It seems he had a mistress to whom he had paid big money
it cost him 250 grand over three years just to call her honey
oh, he did admit to palimony—but he claimed he paid much less
than the quarter million dollar tab for his closet-princess

Somehow I could relate to the lust that got Henry into this fix
resulting in his resignation under pressure in 1996
with more carefully chosen words, he'd have never taken the fall
he could have done like me: just say "I can't recall"

In a fundraiser in Miami, I praised my fallen friend
after his cabinet appointment came to an abrupt end
I alluded to Henry's dedicated public service and distinguished career
too bad it was derailed by a lover turned profiteer

Linda pleaded guilty to 28 charges to avoid a trial
which didn't look good for Henry's wrongdoing denial
if convicted on all charges, she'd have gotten a 140 years
plus fines of up to 4.75 million—for being a sexual racketeer

22

SCANDAL FUNDING

100

WE'RE OFFERING YOU, AT OUR EXPENSE, AN ENDLESS SUPPLY OF READILY AVAILABLE HIGH-PRICED HOOKERS WHO'VE WAIVED ANY ENTITLEMENT TO POTENTIAL LAW SUITS. THIS OFFER IS, OF COURSE, CONTINGENT UPON YOUR SWEARING OFF GOLD DIGGING BIMBOS.
SexLife® Insurance
AFTER FUNDING A MILLION & A HALF IN LEGAL BILLS, AN INSURANCE CO MAKES BILL AN OFFER

P eople weren't comin' off their cash, till Charlie came along
to demonstrate innovative techniques that eventually got the gong
in hundreds of sequentially numbered checks, he provided 460 grand
graced with matching signatures from various cities across the land

It really broke my heart that I had to give it back
I really coulda used the money, but they wouldn't cut me no slack
I was appalled when investigators requested data from Chinese banks
they gave foreign money to me, and that's our nation's *thanks?*

I also dumped my legal bills on some insurance companies
for the mounting debts from Paula and my other calamities
after they funded a million & a half, State Farm said *no mo*
I must have exceeded the liability caps for Presidential libido

When Paula got a fund of her own, her donors were my fair game
figgered I could engage in reprisal once I got each and every name
but the names were off limits to me a Federal Judge would declare
meaning I couldn't harass her supporters; these judges just ain't fair

A pledge was made to bankroll Paula's case by the Rutherford Institute
Why did they chose her side? Why isn't *her* integrity in dispute?
she's just a powerless common-folk; why do they support her cause?
they claimed that even the Prez ain't above the nation's laws

Rutherford has ties with a conservative reverend named Jerry
who once marketed video tapes on me, becoming my adversary
the tapes alleged my connection with (Jerry is so cunning)
multiple murders, financial corruption, and even drug-running

While her financial support was cranking up, mine was winding down
it wasn't putting a dent in my 3 million dollar debt mound
rules imposed by the ethics office really hurt my case
their thousand dollar cap on contributions was a slap in my face

Plus federal employees & lobbyists were prohibited from
giving any money at all to my legal & defense fund
we pulled the plug on the fund; a decision of the trustees
creating a need for new funding to defend my life of sleaze

A new fund was launched thanks to an Arkansan named Dave
he calculated possible debt liquidation if I could learn to behave
he raised my donation cap from one thousand bucks to ten
enabling faster debt recovery so I could start sleazin' again

My new fund raised quick money, targeting those who had it to spare
Hollywood was good for 2 million thanks to each contributing millionaire
but I became concerned about the fund when Kenneth did uncover
evidence that I fibbed under oath about Monica being my lover

My donors had believed in my denials when they donated the jack
but since my testimony wasn't quite the truth, I might have to give it back
because the solicitations for my legal fund were under a false pretense
I should be required to refund all donations and underwrite my own defense

23

THE
PAULA GATE
DEPOSITION

F or $700 grand and my apology
Paula claimed she'd drop her sexual suit against me
but when she turned down our offer to put an end to this mess
the Feds started harassing her, via the IRS

Although these two incidents had no link
Paula's publicist started creatin' a stink
askin *Why audit her? She makes very little dough*
when the White House makes an offer, you shouldn't say "no"

Paula subpoenaed Gennifer for information not revealed
although I once confided in Genny, she has already squealed
imagine them together; two arousing creatures
comparing notes on their memories of my distinguishing features

Gennifer had already blabbed our secrets to a tabloid called *The Star*
after which I went on national television and branded her a "lar"
she then made public the two of us chattin' on audio tape
in which I insulted the Italians, a near fatal scrape

I apologized to Mario & to his ethnic group
but that wasn't the lowest that Gennifer would stoop
she then told all in an adult male magazine
she bared all as well—which I'd already seen

Paula upped the settlement request from 700 grand to 2 mill
but why would I pay a woman who had denied me of my thrill?
so I submitted to the deposition, and I couldn't believe my eyes
this redhead seated across from me—could it be Paula in disguise?

She had a much softer hairstyle than the Paula who rebuffed me
her make-up was toned down, and she looked better I'll agree
the bright red lips were gone, and she'd had her teeth done
perhaps after the deposition, she'll join me in some fun

The deposition wasn't short—it lasted some six hours
they delved into my sexual past and alleged abuse of powers
and y'know, under oath my memory's got much better
'cuz I remembered the affair with Gennifer, right to the letter

Gen was everything I wanted in a woman—and much, much more
she always gave me 100%; what else could I ask for?
yes we had frequent sex; the quality was really great
but I never committed adultery—I didn't ejaculate

COURTROOM MAKE·OVERS

BEFORE

AFTER

BEFORE

AFTER?

24

MONICA AND KATHLEEN

There were questions about a once well-to-do fox named Kathleen
who'd asked me for a paying job; she fallen into the broke scene
so I seized the opportunity to initiate some play
unfortunately her husband committed suicide that very day

I groped and fondled this woman, she would come to claim
but I treated her no differently than I do any other dame
I always wanted to do it, so that's just what I did
but the oval office is not the place for a woman to turn frigid

She got a paid position—it had nothing to do with our encounter
'twas just something my administration coincidentally just found her
but I did say we oughta see if we could do something for this chick
who was seen leaving the oval office, disheveled with smeared lipstick

They wanted to know about Dolly, an old high school classmate
who authored a book about our lengthy affair—heck, we didn't even date!
she claimed she'd received a warning from my Presidential Campaign
that when the tabloids offer to buy her story, she'd better exercise restraint

They also asked me about a farewell encounter on the day I left for DC
in which I met a gal at the Governor's Mansion, as early as could be
we said our goodbyes in the multi-purpose office—actually a private basement nest
for a taxpayer-sanctioned lovers' suite, it was among the very best

They wanted to know about a phrase I used with troopers on detail
describing sexually agressive chicks with whom I was likely to prevail
"that come-hither look" was my desciption to them of such a loose lady
their bringing the "come hithers" to my attention, was admittedly, a tad shady

They wanted to know about Shiela & how many times I bunked at her place
when Hillary wasn't with me, which in this event was the case
I denied having sexual relations with her—how would they ever know
how intimate I was with the co-owner of the Hotel del Coronado?

The questioning went back to Gennifer and her state job I helped arrange
she gave me really great sex, so I got her a position in exchange
"improper" were the findings of the Grievance Review Committee for the state
but they'd have done the same for her—the sex really was that great!

Then they started asking questions about other stuff; it really wasn't fair
like having sex with a young intern—I didn't think they'd care
OK, I bought her really nice gifts including an incredible dress
cuz when I romance a woman, she has to look her best

Y'see, Monica was a California girl when she was referred to me
to be an intern at the White House where she would work for free
I gladly accepted the referral, it came from insurance magnate, Walt
who'd given the DNC & other Dems over 450 grand from his vault

I denied in the deposition to having sex with young Monica
but when Linda turned over her tapes, I appeared moronic . . . duh
she had over 20 hours of tapes with Monica she'd recorded on the sly
that made me out to be a perjurer and an adulterous sort of guy

Monica & I made sure that our deposition statements were a match
so Kenny figured he had me—a suborning perjury catch
but I'd been accused before; no charges ever seemed to stick
I'd fill 'em with doubletalk and charm; 'twas my favorite trick

I was accused of having a relationship about which I asked her to lie
some of the accusations were true—I certainly couldn't deny
on the allegations I did what I do best, I blew a lot of smoke
in an interview with Jim on PBS—I became a national joke

I used double-negatives—a clever use of semantics
to make my admission look like denial; one of my favorite antics
when I said *I never asked anybody not to tell the truth*
I actually meant *I did ask them to;* I learned it in my youth

I'm going to say this again; I want you to listen to me
I did not have sexuals relations with that woman, Miss Lewinsky
the relations we had were special—there was no intercourse
it's OK to have it that way—the Bible is my source

I never told anybody to lie, not a single time
maybe twice, thrice or more—but is that a serious crime?
these allegations are false! Now I've got this to say:
I was relieved that the stain the first dress they tested didn't contain my DNA

I later sealed my lips on our relationship, but you'll never understand
how good some *strange* makes me feel, especially Monica's brand
then as my ratings climbed as high as we've ever seen
I was embarrassed with televised allegations from "groping accuser" Kathleen

But they never got the testimoney from the former Arkansas beauty queen
who, according to deposition, I forced sex on in a limousine
Liz was an eventual Miss America; God she was really cute
she'd fled the country to avoid testimony in Paula's sexual law suit

25

OTHER TRISTS UNVEILED

Then she betrayed her old lover, she admitted we had sex to the press
but she threw in a "consensual" disclaimer, to make it a cleaner sort of
mess
she later apologized to Hillary, for enabling her ol' man to go astray
she should have apologized to me for exposing the way I play

Like the way I played with Beth, a Judge in the Arkansas Municipal Court
she was given a high court appointment after being my sexual cohort
those were the allegations: I advanced careers in exchange for sex
but I thought it was proper as long as no one objects

Did I ever tell you about Debra, the flight attendant on Longhorn One?
the official charter of my Presidential Campaign, on which I had much fun
Debra was blond & beautiful—I couldn't resist rubbing her thighs
so when photographic evidence was published, it wasn't much of a surprise

I had to take care of Debra, because she had the goods on me
she became a receptionist at the White House, where we practice equal
opportunity
then she became the assistant to the State Department's protocol chief
it's better to take care of your woman, than deal with the sexual harrassment
grief

Gettin' back to the Paula trial, a decision from Judge Sue
was that my behavior may have been boorish, if Paula's claims were true
but boorish behavior wasn't against the law in this judge's eyes
so she opted to dismiss the case, much to my surprise

Some of the sexual misconduct testimony made me look really bad
it added to the mountain of evidence prosecutor Kenny already had
he'd been bombarding Vernon with questions about Monica and me
yeah, she made 37 oval office visits, but it was Betty she came to see

Kenny didn't believe my line—I know it was quite lame
and every time I denied a sexual relationship with this dame
the press made me look like tabloid trash—what was I to do?
so I stopped talking 'bout the intern and the other bimbos too

The media would grill me from time to time, but why look like a fool?
I hid behind "executive privilege" to avoid the ridicule
but I'd opened the door one day to questions from the press
and Sam hit me with a blockbuster, I certainly must confess

he acknowledged that my private life sins may be nobody's biz
but when committed by a lesser person, perhaps his or her action is
he asked me if presidential behavior was above the law of the lands
of course I believe the president's is, but I maintained my silent stance

Matt made an internet report of an incident from the past
when the media covered this kinky event, America was aghast
let me sanitize it for you: Yasser stopped in from Palestine
while Monica and I were in the oval office startin' to unwind

I stuck him in the rose garden, although this may sound bizarre
to give me a little time with Monica to enjoy a nice cigar
Monica's not into cigar smoke, so she used it as a toy
to massage her hard-to-reach body parts—and it excited me. OH BOY!

I don't know how Matt gets this stuff, but he's probably the very best
at getting goods on me, like the film of me entering my love nest
with this sweet young gal in her twenties—it wasn't Monica this time
I run a plethora of chics through my study while they're in their prime

The clip started off with a dozen of us, jogging in an event to raise some funds
after which this cutie pie started towelling me off (the fun had just begun)
the group reconvened in the oval office where I signed some autographs
after which I said goodbye to them, leaving a cozy two-person staff

I lead her into my private study where I do my very best work
I guess I could have behaved myself, but my self-control went berzerk
I was pleased to have her as my leading lady, and I was proud to be the star
of the White House documentary filmed from a door that was left ajar

26
FUN ABOARD
AIR-FORCE ONE

One day at L.A. International, I decided to have some fun
I delayed 37 flights on two runways by idling Air Force One
the tie-up cost $76K, but I didn't really care
it seemed like an ideal time to have my stylist do my hair

I called a talk radio show once from aboard Air Force One
whinin' 'bout the bashin's from Rush & G. Gordon
for 23 minutes I questioned their media style & couth
beggin' 'em to lighten up; I'm embarrassed by the truth

I played hearts aboard Air Force One with a female reporter from *Time*
under the table I brushed my foot lightly against Nina's—which ain't no crime
I stared at her legs, and while dealing the cards, I touched her wrist
I had her totally mesmerized, but we never had a trist

Nina later wrote a piece in *Mirabella* supporting my nonsexual harassment way
I'd have obviously scored with that woman—if I'd have only initiated some play
she wrote that *she'd be happy to give me oral sex* . . . (believe me I'd be happy too)
. . . *just to thank me for keeping abortions legal* (is there anything else I can do?)

27

WHITE-WATER GATE

A RARE GROUP PHOTO OF BILL, HILLARY AND THEIR POLITICAL APPOINTEES

W e had entered into a game of monopoly—in the political Arkansas-style
we played with other peoples money, and done so for a while
but Jim & Sue had an unfortunate fate; they played different cards than me
the one they needed most of all was "get out of jail for free"

Our monopoly board consisted of the land around a river
our financier's name was David, and boy could he deliver
like the cozy $300K loan to Sue—we knew it wasn't right
but it helped fund our project—named for the river whose water is white

The Grand Jury subpoenaed Sue for her testimony
I figgered she'd spill the beans on Hill & me
but she refused to testify; the dirt on us was preserved
Sue wasn't so lucky—given jail time to be served

Ever notice that I leave a trail of people who end up dead or in jail?
how I accomplish this is a secret I'll not unveil
I even have the elitists, who give me two for the price of one
like Jim, who got the slammer and died before his time was done

Though in an incarcerated existence, Susan chose to stay alive
so in another Grand Jury appearance, for me she took a second dive
she was mum on a Madison check annotated to pay off me
she got indicted for contempt, and I got off scot-free

While Jim was spoutin' off about me, Sue had sealed her lips
so when fate dealt Jim his unfortunate hand, Sue got better scripts
for her noble acts of silence—indicative of a surviving supporter of mine
we got her released from prison because she had *curvature of the spine*

I'd testified myself that Madison had never given me any loans
so figgered without a doubt I was out of the danger zone
but Madison employee, Henry, left his disabled car for junk
at a repair shop with my $27,000 Madison check in the trunk

Ten years later a mechanic found the check
luckily I never endorsed it, so what the heck?
but I'm still accused of having committed perjury
for merely hiding my financial reconstructive surgery

Things started lookin' bad for the banks that took care of me
they started showin' up at the financial mortuary
they listed me & my cronies as possible beneficiaries
and witnesses of institutional criminal activities

I appointed a crony to reject these references by RTC
to the influential position of U.S. Attorney
an' Paula done real good in an initial wrongdoing efface
but wasted no time recusing herself from the rest of the case

A former associate AG had to serve some time
after pleadin' guilty to partakin' in Whitewater crime
but through new wave financin' he learned from our development corps
Web sleazed another 'half a mill' before reachin' the jailhouse door

He got his windfall from my close friends and supporters
who'd written him checks on their own, not under my orders
some allege that the 'half a mill' bought Webbie's silent tongue
on the Rose Law Firm funny business that Hillary was among

He served a full 18 months for stealing a half mill from Rose
and failing to pay $143 grand in taxes—an option that he chose
but shortly after his discharge from jail, he experienced dejavu:
a tax evasion indictment for him, Suzie, and his tax advisers too

He was charged with failure to pay the $894 grand that he owed
in taxes, interest and penalties—figured he had IRS snowed
he & Suzie paid less than 30 grand in taxes over a period of three years
when their income was over a million—they underpaid, it appears

Along came my friend Vinnie with his financial prowess
workin' on my delinquent taxes & the whole Whitewater mess
he had a wealth of documents incriminating me & my bride
but ended up dead in the park, a suspicious suicide

His sudden passing deterred our further gettin' smeared
cuz the mud-files he had on us mysteriously disappeared
the press soon started buzzin' . . . suggesting impropriety
in the death and missing papers . . . a political conspiracy?

The truth is attorney-client privilege . . . and of course we will not tell
but the high court said that argument was one they would repel
how dare they intervene on my execution of politics
The system ain't even broken . . . and they're insistin' on a fix

I appointed a Judge named James to U.S. District Court
Hell, I had lotsa cronies in trouble; figgered they could use my support
he dismissed the charges on Web & Suzie in 1998
and they were both discharged from prison, in spite of Whitewater Gate

131

28

SCANDAL SOUP

The co-chair of my fitness counsel was an athlete named Flo Jo
But by mid 1997 I wanted to let her go
I'd received $100,000 from fitness guru Jake
He met my donation criterion; Flo didn't—her big mistake

Archer Daniels Midland makes half the ethanol in our land
and chairman Dwayne gave us Democrats a check for a hundred grand
a few days after he tickled my pockets, I decided to make a call
I publicly endorsed and called for the use of more ethanol

We acquired FBI files on prominent Repubs—about 900 strong
they claimed, according to the Privacy Act, what we did was wrong
Judicial Watch sought $90 million for invasion of privacy
heck, I only wanted some dirt on them, cuz they got lots on me

We needed an ambassador to our neighbor, Mexico
and *soft on drugs* was the way I wanted to go
I nominated Willie—he supports the medicinal use of grass
meaning one could legally inhale with a doctor's pass

I liked the prescription weed idea, although Willie's a tad strange
he even supports a program for needle-exchange
but Jesse disappointed me—he said this would not go
he opposed my *drug-friendly* envoy to Mexico

Jesse frustrated Willie, who withdrew as a nominee
insistin' his confirmation shouldn't be acquired on bended knee
I kept my distance from the sparring sessions, but felt bad that Willie failed
but I had my medical prescription ready in case he had prevailed

Luxembourg also needed a U.S. ambassador
so I checked who'd given me money—I'm always keeping score
James had donated to my campaign over $185 grand
add diversity points for being gay—he had to be my man

In a meeting with homosexual lobbyists I promised to set aside
five senior-level positions for gays who were openly bona fide
so when I found myself with a White House management shop to run
My choice was Ginny who qualified as a lesbian former nun

This position was formerly held by my Arkansas buddy, Davey
who fired the entire travel office to give Arkansans their jobs of gravy
too bad for Davey, he done real good till he, too, got fired
for flying the Presidential Copter to a golf course—a practice I admired

For the 9th U.S. Circuit Court of Appeals, James was my nominee
he was already a judge, so I figgered approval would be challenge-free
he claimed to be the teenage brother of a black boy murdered by whites
after it was exposed as a lie, he surrendered his 9th Court sights

After sheep were successfully cloned, I proposed a ban
outlawing the cloning of humans, or any such replication plan
no doubt there could be redeeming results for all the world to see
for instance think of the benefits of having multiples of me

Dan got involved in a House Post Office scandal in 1994
he was indicted for embezzling, witness tampering & more
he pleaded guilty to mail fraud, and was duly put away
in a federal prison where he collected annual retirement of 96K

29

LAND MINES & ASSAULT WEAPONS

In a push for a global land mine ban, I dissented and gave a *no*
I still wanted to use them in Korea—my land mine-support de facto
I know what's best during combat; yes I can relate
from my college campus during the Asian War, I's known to demonstrate

This went against Di's wish; she'd visited victims in the field
but once we fill the VA Hospital, we can still have my *no* repealed
on the subject of banning mines, Jody won the Nobel Peace Prize
the fact that I never congratulated her came as no big surprise

There are reasons for my decisions—reasons you cannot see
reasons with which I don't expect our disabled vets to agree
I can skyrocket the business for undertakers and the prosthetics industry
so why does Jody think I'm on the wrong side of humanity?

Boris then announced Russia's support of Jody's cause
this left only China and the United States giving land-mines their applause
but when Jody announced she'd split with her group the million dollar prize
I considering joinin' for my share of the monetary merchandise

Sticking with my pro-land-mine stance certainly wouldn't have been wise
So I flip-flopped my position, but I did it in disguise
to test my secret turnabout, I called on sweet Madeleine
to announce plans to demine the planet by year 2010

When 120 nations signed the treaty, giving land mines a thumbs-down
I refused to endorse the global ban—I still wanted them around
I can understand why y'all land mine victims disagree with me
cuz if I had to do combat in Korea I'd have supported the ban, you see?

But you'll notice that I was sympathetic to those opposed to guns;
those uncomfortable with neighbors owning assault type weapons
I successfully banned the manufacture and importation
of this type of weaponry into our nation

The National Rifle Association didn't like what I'd done
the 3½ million members felt I was infringing on their fun
they got a new president who lashed out to me
in bold language spelled out with resonant clarity

We Americans didn't trust you with our health care plan
or with gays in the military when you removed the ban
or with our 21 year old daughters, with whom you had so much fun
and we sure, Lord, don't trust you with our guns

30

CHELSEA GATE

When Chelsea entered Stanford, we cut the umbilical cord
she wanted to mix with real people—with us she was gettin' bored
a student columnist wrote an article about her; a practice we had banned
for his audacious efforts, this journalist was duly canned

A second article—this one satire—was written on young Chelsea
in another student newspaper at rival U of C
intended to rally spirit for the football game of these schools
but I figgered he went out of bounds of journalistic rules

So I sicced the Secret Service on this columnist named Guy
who coined me the Sexual Predator in Chief—and I really don't know why
how dare he satirize my daughter and my sexual indiscretions
my agents searched his apartment to teach him a couple lessons

31

MY MEMORIAL LIBRARY & SUPPORT APPRECIATION

I decided to have a memorial established to immortalize my name
to help remind future generations of my political reign of shame
I chose the city of Little Rock to have my presidential library built
funded by an increase in taxes—I'm a man who has no guilt

The 1 cent tax increase was targeted for hotels and restaurants
but my *hamburger-tax* increase received a negative public response
on the issue of increasing taxes, Little Rock citizens weren't on my side
so city officials chose to use bond money that had been already set aside

The money had been earmarked to buy land for golf courses for the city
which will play second fiddle to my library—isn't it a pity?
but I'm sure we'll still get the golf courses, so I can sharpen up my game
we'll just increase the tax on hamburgers—it all comes out the same

I appreciate the biblio-enshrinement; now I'll take my turn
I'd like to express my gratitude to all; even to those who've gotten burned
I'm dedicating these words to y'all because you have all allowed me
to have fun abusing my powers while misleading this country

I'm indebted to my supporters who ended up six feet under
I felt the pain of my cronies when the served time for our blunders
I'd like to acknowledge all my friends who lied to hide my many sins
lyin's OK in politics; it rewards us with undeserved wins

I'd like to thank Ross for screwing up the election
enabling me to win this post—he was my unlikely connection
I'd like to thank y'all taxpayers for funding my sexual escapades
and for the first class accommodations for my bimbo brigades

Plus I'd like to thank the bimbos to whom I put the boots
and thank you to the judges who dismissed my legal suits
a special thanks to my cronies for sealing their lips
and another thanks to y'all taxpayers for all my foreign trips

Y'all remember those excursions on which I took a minor entourage?
the thousand or so of my cronies with whom I shared my bon voyage
no, I didn't need to take them all, but it was my strategy
to give them the tax-funded vacations so they'd feel indebted to me

As long as people owe me favors, it's like money in the bank
and since the favors cost me nothin', I've got y'all tax payers to thank
and it doesn't come cheap for y'all, multi million bucks for each such jaunt
my status as a well-traveled prez is something I like to flaunt

It's expected that my chosen travelers make the best of the opportunity
to travel first class with the president, carving out a part of history
and when it's time to pay me back, this may sound a little funny:
from the gals I'd like to take it out in trade, from the guys I prefer money

One U.S. Trade Representative made good use of her China trip
Charlene picked up forty Beany Babies, obviously counterfeits
she only wanted to check the quality of these Chinese-manufactured toys
she had no intentions to sell these pirated goods to American girls or boys

And yes, we enjoyed the travel, glamour and the glitz
and Hillary enjoyed being your first lady when I wasn't giving her fits
she actually was your president—she was the one who called the shots
I was too busy chasing the interns for whom I had the hots

32

THANK YOU FOR NOT IMPEACHING

C an you believe that 17 conservative House members, led by Bob
had the nerve to introduce a resolution targeting my job
they wanted the judiciary committee to make a determination
whether there's enough office abuse evidence for impeachment consideration

They suggested my decisions are influenced by illegal foreign donations
but I give illegal domestic money the same consideration
I was obstructing congressional investigations was another alleged offense
but we had to take the time to preview the evidence

And Kenneth was convinced that I was doin' lotsa lyin'
he thinks I used the White House for my personal concubine
and to cover-up the adultery your federal taxes were paying for
I asked an intern to lie for me to show she wasn't my White House whore

I'm a politician and attorney—so I'm good at tellin' lies
but when my body guards got subpoenaed, I was worried 'bout those guys
they don't have my Teflon coating, and they're not schooled to tell a fib
so how were they supposed to respond when asked *with whom I shared my crib?*

But I'm very well-connected—I appoint people to high positions
and *they must play my game* is one of the unwritten conditions
if they have loose lips, they might have an unfortunate destiny
count the number in jail or dead who've tried to cross up me

I was a tad surprised that William gave the green light
for the Secret Service to give testimony—it really wasn't right
I should have gotten a judge who felt totally indebted to me
for his or her judgeship appointment, so I could be home free

But I never appointed William; he's the one who swore me in
he didn't owe me nothin', so how was I supposed to win?
I couldn't get special consideration, so I had to keep tellin' lies
but I don't consider it perjury; merely the truth presented in disguise

Monica's new counsel struck an immunity deal
blowing the pledge that our intimacy was something we'd conceal
so I played my ace-in-the-whole when she was scheduled to testify
I sent her a televised signal by sporting her gift neck tie

She either didn't get my signal or she just presented the facts
I never thought she'd tell the truth—after all, we had a pact
and then she added to my predicament another colossal mess
she toted a bag into the courtroom containing the famous souvenir dress

I thought the first dress they tested cleared me of causing a stain
her mother stored this dirty garment; what's up with her brain?
I'd already agreed to testify, but I didn't know what to say
I considered "I had an accident while crossdressing in which I squirted DNA"

In my Grand Jury testimony, which is actually nobody's biz
I challenged the meaning of words—like what's the definition of "is"?
and by *my* definitions, we neither had sex nor were we ever alone
I was lost for words, though, when asked if we ever had sex on the phone

In this ultimately televised testimony, I recanted my previous quips
that Monica and I never had any improper relationships
to make peace with my constituents, I then made a public address
this all would have been unnecessary if Monica had washed her dress

I used Bill-buzzwords throughout, in my patented vernacular
and I never apologized to anybody—I thought I was spectacular
I asserted that I was legally accurate in my January deposition
when I denied having an affair with Monica in my deceptive tradition

I admitted to having an inappropriate relationship with her
    [duh..but not a sexual affair?]
it constituted a critical lapse in judgement I would publicly declare
Monica was livid about the words I used in my eloquent address
she'd inferred from our trist that we were in love, which I didn't confess

When she testified again, she was a woman scorned
I was concerned that in her anger she'd claim her perjury was suborned
Kenneth called her back because our testimonies just didn't jibe
perhaps the passive role I'd claimed was not what she'd described

While we were fully clothed we engaged in some fondling
but that's not sexual relations—just a touchy-feely thing
then we'd both proceed in a manner I'd schooled her in:
as long as we followed my prescription of love, I wasn't engaging in sin

I assumed a passive role while she performed fellatio on me
since we avoided the missionary position, it was technically sodomy
sodomy isn't intercourse—I learned that in Arkansas
and if it was legally considered sex, I'd have just amended the law

Now we get to the important part; this is really great!
while in rapture over Monica's efforts, I didn't ejaculate
she would terminate her performance when I got close to ecstasy
I'd then gratify myself in the excitement that she provided for me

Now you must admit that in a legal sense, I didn't engage in sex
which would clear me of the perjury that Kenneth's team suspects
what I described can be construed as normal office activity
for which I, as a virile male, have a bustling proclivity

And if it fits one's definition of sex, y'all would have to agree
I didn't have sex with Monica; she had sex with me
she might have claimed there were a few times when my timing wasn't great
that wasn't sex either—I just happened to prematurely ejaculate

After my Monday night public address, I needed some time to heal
I retreated to Martha's Vineyard for what little time I could steal
my family seclusion was shortened because of something I had planned:
to launch a missile attack on Sudan and Afghanistan

The bombing took the focus off my scandal of sex and lies
but it was life imitating art, the conservatives would criticize
I thought the strategy of *wagging the dog* was tastefully deceptive
and if y'all hadn't seen the movie, you'd have been a little more receiptive

After plagiarizing the waggin' strategy, I took a little trip
to visit another wounded leader at the 2-day Moscow summit
with no domestic US press to dog me, I figured I'd unwind
but it was dejavu in Moscow; the media was less than kind

The Kremlin should have been a sanctuary for me to lick my festered wound
but they questioned me about Monica, and I came off like a buffoon
I explained to them that I'd made peace at home via my public address
in which I asked to be "forgiven" for the "mistake" that got me in this mess

For being put on the spot by reporters, I thought I did just great
with the concise spontaneous answer I managed to articulate
but my Monday night address did not contain (I was later told)
either word I expressed in Moscow—fitting my jive-talk mold

I didn't wanna go home and face the music yet, so I made an interim stop
figgered I could get some sympathy in Ireland by flaunting a Clinton tear drop
but, NO! The reporters asked me to comment on the words expressed by Joe
the senator who wouldn't accept my affair as presidential status quo

Y'all saw through all my jive-talk, and I'd run out of spin
I finally had to apologize, much to my chagrin
it really hurt me deeply to say "I made a bad mistake"
you'll notice I kept *mistake* singular; it's all my ego could take

"It's indefensible..." I admitted (so why should I have fought)
"...and I'm sorry about it" (I'm sorry I was caught)
I'd have probably gotten away with it, but for Paula's sexual harassment case
if I'd have initially apologized to Paula, I wouldn't have this public disgrace

Suddenly Paula wanted her case reheard (maybe now I'll apologize)
because my testimony regarding Monica might have been full of lies
conservatives called for a contempt hearing—claiming I lied about sex
but I'm innocent because we had sodomy—they're dealing with intellects

I then focused on my private life, which I intended to reclaim
which became quite difficult considering my extramarital shame
I still planned to finish my term of office to keep my legacy intact
but my reputation got more shaky as 36 boxes were unpacked

Kenneth had filled these cardboard boxes with evidence supporting
his 455 page document about my oval office cavorting
David fired back a rebuttal (he's a clairvoyant dude)
before he'd even seen the document (his telepathic feud)

I started apologizing to everyone, including my favorite intern
then David came to my defense (he didn't want me to burn)
he insisted I committed no perjury, nor did I exercise power abuse
nor did I tamper with any witnesses—he was trying to uncook my goose

The report exposed my impeachable acts (eleven separate grounds)
it was posted on the internet, which I thought was out of bounds
it provided all my sexual encounters in extremely lurid detail
I immediately considered my new defense: I was a sexually-addicted male

The evidence was overwhelming, including my matching DNA
my lying wouldn't work any more—contradicting testimony was on display
I was looking more and more like expresident tricky Dick
but I held another ace in the whole; that's why they call me "slick"

Kenneth's referral to the House of Representatives read like a Hollywood script
and since I was the philanderer this scandalous writing did depict
when I am your expresident, I plan to start collecting a royalty
for the book and movie rights to the *Scandals of Slick Willy*

I'll be moving to Hollywood in pursuit of my new career
where my good buddy Steven will help turn me into a profiteer
nobody else could accurately portray this scoundrel, don't y'all see?
the leading role of the disgraced president is custom made for me

RESOURCES

BOOKS

BOY CLINTON The Political Biography by R. Emmett Tyrrell, Jr.
PASSION & BETRAYAL by Gennifer Flowers
SLEEPING WITH THE PRESIDENT by Gennifer Flowers

Newspapers

Baltimore Sun
Delaware State News
National Liberty Journal
News Journal (Wilmington)
New York Times
Richmond Times
Sun Sentinal
USA Today
Washington Post
Washington Times National Weekly Edition

Magazines

Biography
CQ Researcher
Insight on the News
MacLeans
Newsweek
People
Time

Television

ABC News: *Freeloaders with John Stossel*

Videotape

A prescription for Disaster: What the Clinton Health Care Plan Means for You
        presented by Jerry Falwell

Internet

The Drudge Report

Other

The Falwell Fax

YOUR CLINTON SCANDAL QUOTIENT

Thank you for reading *The Clinton Scandals*. It is no secret that this title, with its format of cartoon-illustrated poetry, challenges the industry standard on political books. It is also by no accident that the cast of characters is presented in the context of the poetry without last names. This renders the entire book a lengthy cryptogram from which one is able to test his or her knowledge on the Clinton scandals. Your *Clinton Scandal Quotient* can be determined through a CSQ test. To administer this test to yourself, simply turn to the *Sindex* (a guide for locating characters in the Clinton Sea of Sin) on the next two pages, and identify the Clinton cast of characters listed alphabetically by their first names. Proper character identification is nothing more than providing the correct last name for each first name. Divide the number of characters you accurately identified by the number of characters in the *Sindex*. The resulting percentage is your Clinton Scandal Quotient (CSQ). No cheating.

SINDEX

guide for locating characters in the Clinton sea of sin

AUTHOR BIO

Bill Whitaker was raised in northern Delaware, an area historically rich in art. His grandfather, who was from the Howard Pyle era, painted masterfully in oils. William W. Whitaker's art included pirates, in the tradition of Howard Pyle, as well as animals in the wild. To emulate his grandfather Bill took up oil painting and filled his walls with pirates and nature scenes of his own. He later began dabbling in cartoons.

He sold some of these cartoons to magazines, and marketed others internationally through a California-based syndicate. A businessman entering a senatorial race recruited Bill to draw cartoons for his campaign, bashing a longtime incumbent through newspaper-published cartoons. The incumbent won, but not before feeling the power of political cartoons. Bill feels cartooning is more creative than painting, but occasionally he combines both art forms (see cover) for a full-color cartoon.

With a growing family and other interests, Bill took a sabbatical from art for about 10 years. He then blew the dust off his drawing board for an even bigger challenge than freelance cartooning: to write and illustrate *White Male Applicant: An Affirmative Action Exposé,* complete with bibliography, endnotes and index. And yes, he managed somehow to include a pirate cartoon in the book. Did I mention that he also did the cover design & photography?

The transition from affirmative action to presidential politics to create this book was quite easy for Bill. But he thought it would be a shame to present it through traditional prose because of all the natural humor in the Clinton administration. He considered satirical poetry with political caricatures, but he wasn't sure if such a book had ever been written about a president. Bill is sure of one thing, though. One has been written now.

ORDER FORM

Please send _____ copies of

_____ *The Clinton Scandals: Political Satire in Cartoon-Illustrated Poetry* ($14.95) By William A. Whitaker

_____ *White Male Applicant: An Affirmative Action Exposé* ($14.95) By William A. Whitaker

_____ send me information on your full color Clinton posters, T shirts of the cover art, and other ancillary products

to:

Name_____

Street Address_____

City_____ State_____ Zip:_____–_____

Telephone:_____

• Price: $14.95 per copy

• Shipping & Handling $2.00 for first book and 75 cents for each additional book mailed at the book rate. Priority rate is $3.00 per book

• Payment: provide check or money order to cover the cost of the purchase and shipping. Mail payment to the mailing address listed below.

• Apropos Press (postal address)
PO Box 118
Smyrna, DE 19977-0118

• Apropos Press E Mail Address: APROPRESS@aol.com

• Apropos Press Web Page: http://www.bookzone.com (enter book title at site)

• Apropos Press Fax: 1 (302) 653-2132